# THE STEP BY STEP ART OF
# *Flower Arranging*

CLB 2711
This edition published 1992 by Colour Library Books
© 1992 Colour Library Books Ltd, Godalming Surrey
Printed and bound in Singapore
All rights reserved
ISBN 0 86283 950 5

# THE STEP BY STEP ART OF
# *Flower Arranging*

Text by
JANE NEWDICK

Photography By
NEIL SUTHERLAND

Colour Library Books

# Contents

# First Things First
## A Practical Guide to Preparing and Conditioning Flowers

*Before you begin working with flowers, there are a few practical points to be aware of. It helps if you know which are the right tools to choose and how to get the very best out of the materials that you will be using. One or two basic techniques, such as wiring dried flowers or rescuing blooms that look less than happy, are useful to know so that with a few simple skills at your fingertips you will be able to make any of the arrangements in this book.*

*A range of materials and tools for working with dried flowers.*

Above: *Iceland poppies need boiling water to seal their stems.*

Fresh flowers will repay a little time and effort spent on their preparation with a long and colourful life in an arrangement. If you buy flowers from a good market stall or flower shop the chances are that they will have been conditioned. This means that stems will have been cleaned of foliage and re-cut, then stood in water for several hours to have a long drink. The stems on flowers bought in a bunch out of water will have dried and possibly sealed over and will need to be cut again and given a drink. Flowers picked from a garden should also be given this preparatory treatment, preferably in the evening or early morning, which are the best times of day to gather material before too much moisture has transpired from the plant. Normal soft stems should be cut at a long slant to give the largest surface area possible to absorb water. A few very large flowers, such as delphiniums and amaryllis, have hollow stems which can be packed with a small plug of damp cotton wool to help them to drink.

Some flowers and foliage have stems that need to be seared or sealed to prevent them drooping or dropping petals. Poppies are one variety that needs to have this done. Each stem should be held over a flame for a few seconds or stood in a shallow depth of boiling water for two or three minutes. Other varieties that need the heat treatment are euphorbia and some ferns.

Boiling water can also revive wilting stems of flowers such as tulips, sunflowers, gerbera and mallow. A small amount of boiling water is poured into a narrow-necked container and the flowers are stood in this until they are revived.

Any foliage that is not wanted on a stem, or that will be below water, should be removed. Submerged leaves rapidly cloud the water and make it smell and look unpleasant in a clear container. Some flowers, such as stocks and chrysanthemums, should always have stems clear of foliage that might rot.

Above: *Always re-cut stems on a long slant.*

Left: *Clear unwanted foliage from green stems.*

Many flowers and most of the foliage used in flower arranging comes from shrubby plants with strong stems which need slightly different treatment from soft-stemmed annual or herbaceous flowers. Flowers such as lilac are cut from large shrubs or small trees and their stems have bark over a solid woody stem. Preparation of this sort of material is necessary to get the best from it. The base of the stems should be cut on a slant and the bark can be scraped or peeled back a little way to expose the stem beneath. Then either split the stem by cutting a few slices upwards with sharp secateurs or a gardening knife, or hammer the bottom few centimetres with a mallet.

Once more it is important to remove unwanted leaves and small, twiggy branches that might get in the way of the rest of the arrangement or that otherwise would stand under water. Give all woody-stemmed material a good, long conditioning drink in water at room temperature and leave in a cool place until you need to use it. Some foliage can be completely submerged in water for several hours, which makes it very crisp and unlikely to wilt later. Leaves such as beech, hornbeam, and whitebeam, which you might use in a large-scale arrangement, benefit very much from this type of treatment. A large container is obviously required and a bath is usually the best place to do this conditioning.

Above left: *Stripping thorns from a rose stem.*
Above right: *Splitting the base of a woody stem with secateurs.*

Roses need much the same treatment, but if they have large or sharp thorns it is sensible to remove these before trying to arrange them. Roses bought from a flower shop will usually have been de-thorned and nowadays many varieties are thornless. It is a slow job cutting off each thorn, but you can try running a blade or special tool along the stem, rubbing off the thorns as you go. Roses can suddenly and dramatically wilt for no apparent reason, but can often be saved by re-cutting stems and standing in boiling water.

If you plan to work with dried flowers you will need a few extra materials and equipment apart from good sharp florists' scissors or secateurs. Buy some small snips or wire cutters and use these to cut stub or rose wire – do not be tempted to use your secateurs instead. A reel of fine rose wire will be needed, as well as stiff stub wire which is sold ready cut in a choice of lengths and usually by weight.

There is a wonderful range of dried flowers to buy, but you can also dry your own as well as growing your own if you have a garden. Many flowers can be easily dried by hanging bunches in a warm airy atmosphere until crisp and completely free of moisture. Certain varieties of flowers, such as larkspur and achillea, are ideal for this. Other varieties are papery dry as they are harvested and need little treatment. Some, such as helichrysum, however, have very weak stems and are best pushed onto a stiff wire that will rust into the flower and form a new stem.

Whole flower heads can also be dried in a special desiccant that preserves the shape and colour of each bloom very well, though again a wire stem will need to be attached to the flower head for arrangements.

Above: *Many types of flower can be successfully air-dried.*

A glue gun is a useful tool for working with dried flowers, especially for attaching whole seed pods or flower heads to a wreath or the edge of a basket. There is a wide choice of special foam bases in many shapes for use with dried material and apart from cones, rings and balls, you can always cut foam to any shape you choose for free form decorations.

Left: *Perfect flower heads being prepared to be dried in a desiccant.*

Above: *A looped stub wire being attached to a helichrysum head.*

# Special Occasions

There are often times when flower arrangements need to be spectacular. For example you might want to decorate the house for a party or celebration, a special homecoming or anniversary, or for one of the traditional festivals that most of us celebrate at some time during the year. This is a time to be a bit more extravagant than usual and to attempt decorations on a larger scale, perhaps. It may be enough just to choose a bigger container than normal and pick flowers that are larger and more formal than general, or colour could be the key to making something showstopping without spending more money or time than you might for an everyday type of arrangement. The actual arrangements will depend on whether your celebration focuses around a dining or buffet table, or whether you are having a gathering of people standing in one room or using the whole house. Consider such points first, then plan where to put flowers for maximum impact and practicality.

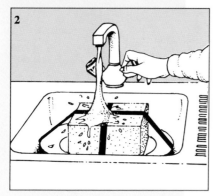

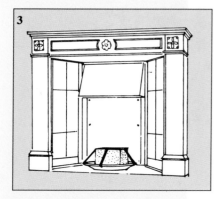

1 Tape foam to a waterproof base or plate. Use special sticky tape sold for this purpose and be sure to wrap it round and under an edge to hold foam firmly.

2 Soak the whole construction in a sink or large bucket. Follow foam manufacturers' instructions for immersion time.

3 Stand the foam in its final position and work in situ if possible, rather than trying to move the final arrangement.

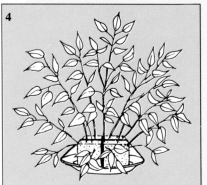

◄ *A magnificent setting such as this marble fireplace demands a lavish flower arrangement. Here the unusual colour combination of hydrangea, lilies, chillies and euphorbia makes a stunning display.*

▲ *Flowers which are to be seen from above are best arranged in situ, as in this fireplace arrangement of gerbera, lilies, irises and generous amounts of flowering shrubs and mixed foliage.*

**4** *Make a basic shape using foliage or stiff-stemmed shrubs or flower spikes. Bring some stems forward out from the foam almost at floor level.*

**5** *Add any solid flower heads at this stage, distributing them evenly throughout the arrangement and keeping them within the outline shape.*

**6** *Add lilies and arching flower sprays throughout the arrangement, filling any gaps.*

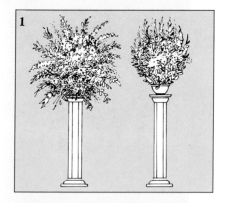

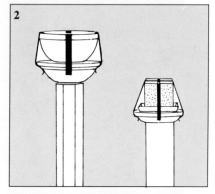

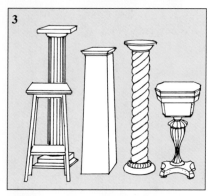

**1** *Always make use of the height of a pedestal by arranging stems to curve downwards rather than in a stiff, upward outline.*

**2** *Be sure to tape the container or block of foam securely to the top of the pedestal and try to keep the centre of gravity low.*

**3** *There are many different styles of ready-made pedestals, both modern and old fashioned. Tall tables or plant stands work just as well, too.*

▶ *A really sumptuous but simple arrangement made using white scented* Lilium longiflorum *mixed with grey-green eucalyptus foliage and the spikey umbrella-shaped leaves of papyrus. The plain, modern white pillar looks exactly right for this style of arrangement.*

▼ *Smaller in scale but far more detailed than the two larger arrangements, this ambitious mixture of white lilac, freesias, hyacinths, chrysanthemums, ranunculus, gerbera and sprays of prunus blossom looks perfect on its pedestal, which is actually a fine antique workbox.*

◀ *Pedestal arrangements are definitely for special occasions. They can use a great deal of plant material but always look spectacular. The mechanics of the arrangement must be good and the pedestal heavy and firm so that the flowers are not likely to fall over. Gerbera, genista and antirrhinum make a superb spring mix.*

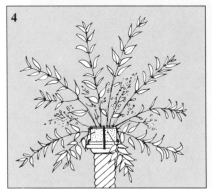

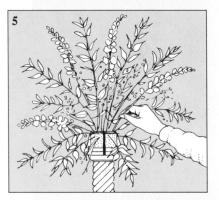

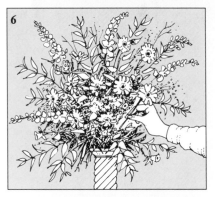

**4** *Always begin a pedestal arrangement by setting the size and outline with solid shapes of foliage or filler material.*

**5** *Fill in with more long-stemmed material, bringing plenty out towards the front of the arrangement.*

**6** *Finally, add the important blooms and smaller material to make a balanced overall effect without empty areas.*

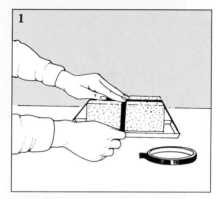

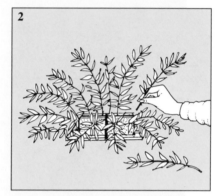

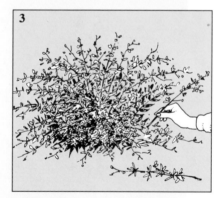

**1** *Use a block or two of damp floral foam as a heavy base for the orchid arrangement. Make sure it stands on a waterproof base.*

**2** *Begin with a filler of foliage to cover the foam and make a solid centre.*

**3** *Work all round the foam, pushing in the stems of orchid and aiming to make a dense, low shape.*

▶ *One very effective but simple way to make a special arrangement is to use a single type of flower but in a large quantity. This always manages to look extravagant and eye-catching, but it is simple to put together. Here a long oak refectory table has been filled with a low but full arrangement of small-flowered vivid red orchids.*

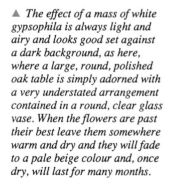

▲ *The effect of a mass of white gypsophila is always light and airy and looks good set against a dark background, as here, where a large, round, polished oak table is simply adorned with a very understated arrangement contained in a round, clear glass vase. When the flowers are past their best leave them somewhere warm and dry and they will fade to a pale beige colour and, once dry, will last for many months.*

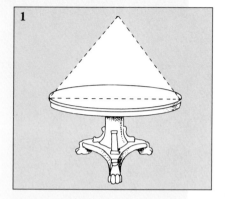

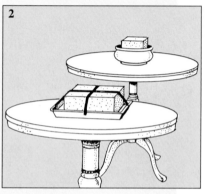

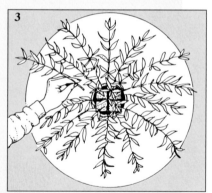

**1** For an arrangement which may be top-heavy cut a square of wire mesh and crumple it to fit the neck of the vase.

**2** Push the wire into the vase, leaving some of it higher than the rim. Use it alone or put it over floral foam inside the vase.

**3** Put thick or woody stems through the wire mesh to keep them in place and held securely.

◀ *A cool and classic combination of white and green always looks sophisticated but fresh. It is a useful colour scheme to use in dark surroundings where many colours would simply disappear against the background. Here white honesty is put with pure white tulips.*

▶ *A fabulous mixture of dozens of different flowers is like a celebration of summer. Many of the flowers are garden grown, while others are more exotic and available only from the florist. This large-scale arrangement would make a stunning focal point in a room to be used for a party or celebration.*

▶ *A rich textural arrangement of summer flowers stands in a classic urn-shaped vase. Crumpled wire is put in the neck of the container to help support the long and top-heavy stems of larkspur, lilac, delphiniums, stocks and aquilegia.*

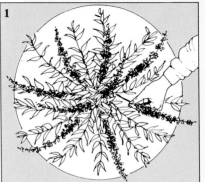

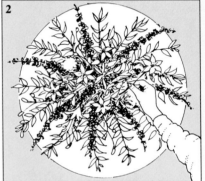

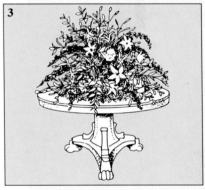

**1** *Put damp foam and crumpled wire in the vase as described. Start to add the main flowers throughout the vase.*

**2** *Put sprays of the filler flowers amongst the main blooms, keeping them in the same plane and within the outline already set.*

**3** *Finally, add a little extra greenery deeper into the arrangement, where it is needed, to act as a foil to the flowers.*

**1** *Begin by making a good solid base from floral foam, or use a shallow container filled with foam.*

**2** *Aim to fill a space with flowers which is roughly conical in shape above the top of the table.*

**3** *Looking from above, begin with a regular covering of foliage stems in a circle against the table surface.*

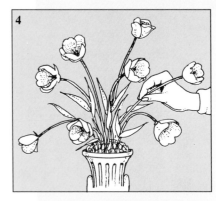

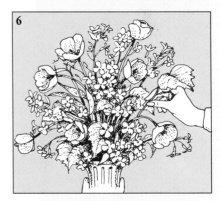

▲ Sometimes a large arrangement can be put onto a round table and designed to be viewed from all angles. This is obviously extravagant with plant material but makes a very spectacular effect for a special occasion. Here lilies, euphorbia and protea combine with richly coloured autumn foliage.

▶ A small, round pedestal table has been completely filled with an arrangement that can be viewed from all directions. A vase or container isn't necessary with this type of design, where the lowest stems practically rest on the table surface.

◀ An elegant and well-proportioned hall demands a splendid, large-scale arrangement to complement it. Choose large, simple blooms which are easily seen from a distance and avoid small, fussy flowers and foliage which simply merge together.

4 Continue to fill the imaginary conical outline with foliage and then add some of the longer flowering stems.

5 Now begin to put in larger blooms and spread them throughout the arrangement to get an even effect.

6 The finished arrangement should have some stems gently curving down and maybe some breaking against the edge of the table.

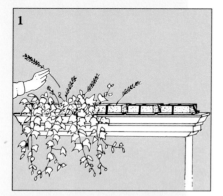

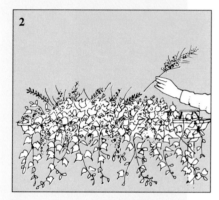

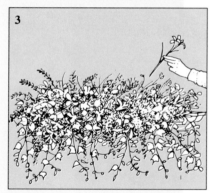

**1** *Stand a row of foam blocks in plastic trays along the shelf and tape them firmly in position. Cover the foam with ivy, letting some trail forward and down.*

**2** *Add sprays of yellow mimosa and short stems of yellow chrysanthemums along the whole length of the shelf.*

**3** *Finally, add the white irises in amongst everything else, spacing them out evenly through the yellow and green.*

*Decorating a mantelpiece is a superb way of making a focal point in a room. Although there is always very little space in which to create something, the flowers and foliage can be allowed to fall naturally forward to break against the edges of the mantel shelf.*

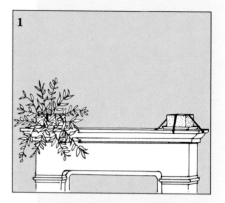

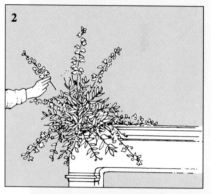

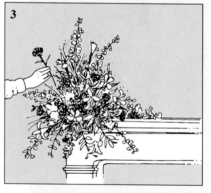

Arranging two matching flower decorations at either end of a mantelpiece leaves the picture on the wall behind unobscured. Here white irises are combined with rich red carnations and blue delphiniums in a patriotic colour scheme.

**1** Tape a block of foam on a plastic tray on each end of the mantel shelf. Begin to add foliage.

**2** Add the long spikes of delphinium in a wheel shape and then add the white irises.

**3** Finish of by adding the red carnations evenly spaced throughout the arrangements.

**1** *You will need, ideally, a stemmed dish or compotier. Pile with decorative fruit.*

**2** *Tuck in amongst the fruit short stems of evergreen leaves in small bunches.*

**3** *Finally, put short stems of roses and alstroemeria in amongst the fruit and leaves. This will last for an evening or more.*

32

▲ *During autumn there is plenty of free material to use for flower arrangements. Look out for sprays of rosehips and branches of berries to add to the vibrant reds and oranges of garden flowers.*

◄ *In winter, when flowers are scarce, make use of glossy evergreen foliage and luscious fruit to create a spectacular table centrepiece for a party, special occasion, or during Christmas festivities.*

▶ *A wonderfully full and varied arrangement of summer flowers which is really only possible if you grow plenty of material in your own garden. An empty fireplace in summer needs an extravagant and beautiful way to conceal it.*

**1** *Pack vase with damp foam and add crumpled wire if you wish. Put tall stems of foliage in place, fanning out the shape.*

**2** *Next add the solid sedum flowers and sprays of berries and rosehips.*

**3** *Finish by putting in the orange marigolds and helichrysums and three stems of pink larkspur.*

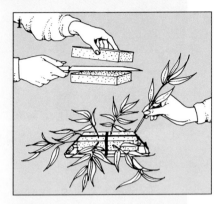

▶ *The soft drapes of old rose-pink curtains provide a backdrop for a romantic arrangement of creamy blush roses and eucalyptus foliage for a pretty table setting for a dinner a deux.*

▼ *A wide, low arrangement of crimson amaranthus, bromeliads, eucalyptus and other exotic foliage, in startling juxtaposition to the classic furnishing and striped sofa in this elegant drawing room.*

**1** *For a low arrangement like this, slice a foam block in half horizontally. Soak it and put it in a waterproof tray. Begin to place the foliage.*

**2** *Next put the solid flower heads in place, aiming for a regular round shape.*

**3** *Lastly, place the roses throughout the arrangement, spacing them very regularly amongst the other material.*

▶ *A scheme of three separate arrangements designed to be seen as a whole makes superb use of a large, built-in storage area. The gerbera give the impact needed on such a big scale, as smaller flowers would be lost amongst so much other material.*

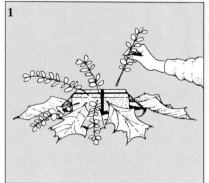

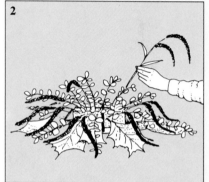

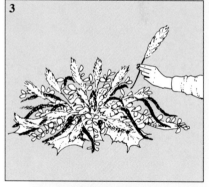

**1** *Put a block of damp foam into a tray or shallow container and tape firmly. Put foliage all round the base.*

**2** *Finish putting eucalyptus over foam and add amaranthus between the leaves.*

**3** *Finally, put the bromeliads in place, spacing them out evenly and keeping to a low, curved outline.*

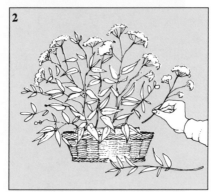

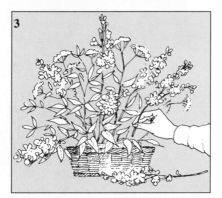

**1** *Line the large shallow basket with foil or plastic and wedge in damp foam to fill it. Begin to set the outline of the shape with foliage and fennel flowers.*

**2** *Add the long stems of stocks in a fan shape, with one facing forward.*

**3** *Now add everything else in any order. Roses, carnations, and alstroemeria should be well mixed throughout the arrangement.*

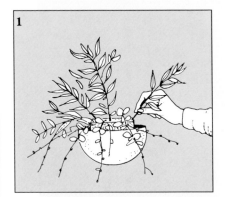

1

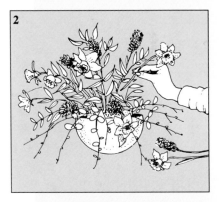

2

3

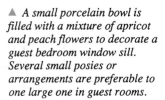

▲ *A small porcelain bowl is filled with a mixture of apricot and peach flowers to decorate a guest bedroom window sill. Several small posies or arrangements are preferable to one large one in guest rooms.*

▶ *A guest bathroom is the location for a beautiful spring bowlful of daffodils and ranunculus, hyacinths and genista. As well as ensuring that they look pretty, make flower arrangements for guests sweetly scented if possible as this is very welcoming.*

◀ *A splendid country-style arrangement in pale colours is thrown into strong relief by its background of a handsome, richly coloured woven carpet. The flowers include cream stocks, white honesty, honeysuckle, cream roses, alstroemeria and spray carnations.*

**1** *Pack a small, round bowl with damp foam and begin to add sprays of foliage and genista.*

**2** *Next add the hyacinth heads and daffodils, spreading them throughout the arrangement.*

**3** *Lastly add the ranunculus, mixing them in amongst everything else.*

# Everyday Arrangements

*However busy you are, a simple arrangement or two makes a big difference to how a house looks and feels. Try to find time to put together a quick bunch of cheerful flowers for a kitchen table and something welcoming in the hall or living room. These arrangements do not need to be elaborate, but should provide a splash of colour – something fresh and alive – and if possible add the bonus of a delicious scent.*

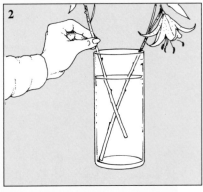

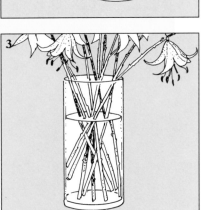

▶ *Nothing could be simpler than a tall, clear glass cylinder vase used to display several stems of the exquisite and highly scented lily Stargazer. The lilies arrange themselves as the stems fall into place.*

▼ *This apricot and blue arrangement looks quite elaborate but in fact needs no mechanics, all the stems being self-supporting. The vivid green of the early beech foliage contrasts well with pale peach roses and bluebells mixed with Queen Anne's Lace.*

**1** *Cut the stems of all the lilies to the same length, keeping them as long as possible.*

**2** *Start by putting just one stem in place, following this with a second one leaning the opposite way.*

**3** *Continue adding the rest of the stems, crossing them to lock them into place and spreading the lilies right round the vase equally.*

▶ *An old-fashioned cream china jug makes a perfect container for a mixture of early summer flowers including sweet peas, ranunculus, honeysuckle, larkspur, anemones, bouvardia and Michaelmas daisies.*

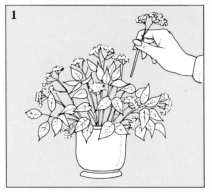

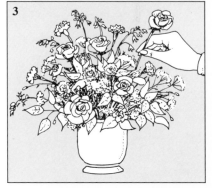

**1** *Fill a vase with water. Put the stems of beech and Queen Anne's Lace in place, spreading them out evenly.*

**2** *Next add bluebell stems, arranging them throughout the foliage and aiming for a full but even effect.*

**3** *Finish off with roses and spray carnations, with the blooms facing toward the front of the arrangement as far as possible.*

# Everyday Arrangements

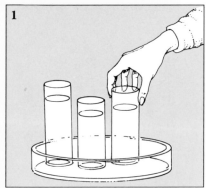

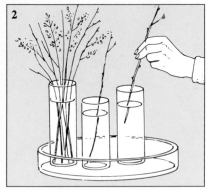

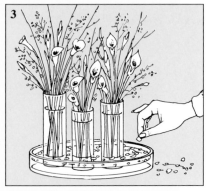

**1** Stand three clear glass cylinders or drinking glasses in a large, round shallow glass dish. Fill the glasses with water.

**2** Put the twigs in place first, followed by the sprigs of genista, mixing them equally throughout the three containers.

**3** Finally add the yellow calla lilies. Pour some water into the shallow round dish and float genista flowers on the surface.

◀ *This stunning golden yellow arrangement is sophisticated but simple. Once you have the right containers and choice of flowers, it is simplicity itself to put together. The colour scheme has been very carefully chosen to work in this particular room but the idea would look equally good in pink or red.*

▶ *Peachy pink gerbera have marvellous stiff stems which stay just where you put them. Placed in a narrow-necked container they need no other mechanics and make a bold modern statement here in contrast to a pretty, florally decorated bedroom.*

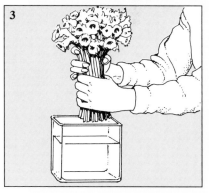

▲ *Pale apricot tulips need no adornment apart from being teamed with a contrasting almond green jug. Tulips are unusual in that they continue to grow and move once picked and put in water, and this needs to be allowed for in the way that they are arranged.*

▶ *Flowers of a single variety often look best used simply and without any extra material. Here golden sunny daffodils are cut to the same length and packed quite tightly into a classic oblong glass tank container. This treatment can be used with other flowers too.*

**1** *Take all the flowers in your hand and cut off the bottom of the stems to make them an equal length. Fill the tank with water.*

**2** *Take all the flowers in one hand, or both if the stems are very thick.*

**3** *Put the bunch into the tank of water and make sure the stems are all touching the bottom. Loosen out the flower heads if they seem to be too bunched together.*

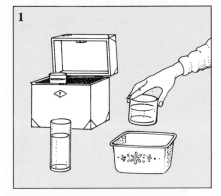

**1** *Many different kinds of containers can be used to hold flowers, and even if they are not waterproof, an inner liner can be improvised.*

**2** *Keep the stems of the flowers fairly long for the larger container and trim them very short for the lower dish.*

**3** *Put longer-stemmed flowers in the main container and leave heads quite loose. Put the very short stemmed blooms in the dish in front.* _____

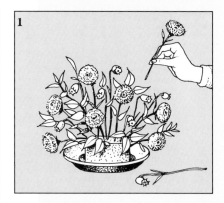

◀ *Unlikely objects can be pressed into service as vases as long as can you find a way to line them or conceal a container with water in it. Here a small wooden box has been filled with a mixture of garden pansies and violas which are standing in water inside glass jars hidden in the box.*

▶ *All kinds of unusual containers can be used to make interesting arrangements. A silver cornucopia is the perfect foil for the brilliant velvety petals of a bunch of mixed anemones. Remember that a group of two or more small arrangements can give much more visual impact than one on its own.*

◀ *A small, richly coloured arrangement for a corner or a hall table. To save on space, a small group of flowers like this can be put into a foam base rather than a proper vase or container as long as it stands in a waterproof tray to protect polished surfaces.*

**1** *Stand a soaked block of floral foam in a tray or dish. Begin with any foliage and the small red dahlias.*

**2** *Add alstroemeria and larger dahlia blooms, keeping a balanced shape to the whole arrangement.*

**3** *Finish off with the red rose stems, spreading them evenly throughout the arrangement and facing them forward for maximum impact.*

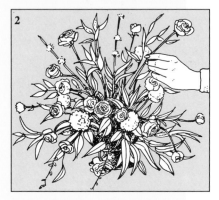

**1** Put a block of damp floral foam in a small, low vase. Put in foliage and stems of viburnum first to set the size of the arrangement.

**2** Next add all the ranunculus, mixing them throughout the arrangement as evenly as possible and filling any gaps.

**3** Finally add the lilies nearer the centre of the flowers and then add the large gerbera blooms, spacing them evenly.

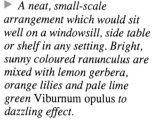

◄ *A very delicate and lacy mixture of blue love-in-a-mist, anemones, Queen Anne's Lace, Michaelmas daisies and rue foliage simply arranged in a stemmed glass goblet – perfect for a bedside table, dressing table or any small space.*

► *A neat, small-scale arrangement which would sit well on a windowsill, side table or shelf in any setting. Bright, sunny coloured ranunculus are mixed with lemon gerbera, orange lilies and pale lime green* Viburnum opulus *to dazzling effect.*

▼ *Stark simplicity comes from this modern black glass vase contrasting with the deep golden yellow of ornamental chillies, a few chrysanthemum heads and orange rosehips. A few pieces of bear grass make graphic curving lines out of the arrangement.*

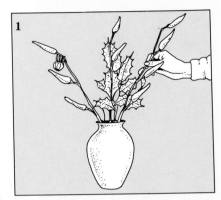

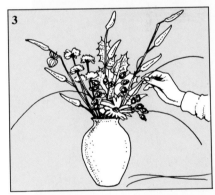

**1** *Fill the vase with water, place one bold piece of foliage at the back and add the stems of chillies on either side.*

**2** *Add pieces of rosehip and then the chrysanthemum sprays still within the outline set by the taller stems.*

**3** *Add the final large chrysanthemum bloom and then the bear grass – one piece on one side and three on the opposite side.*

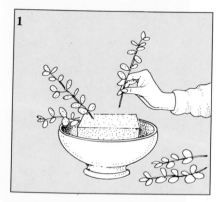

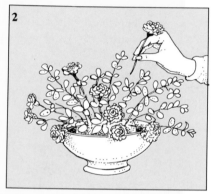

▶ *A 50s lustre bowl sponged pink with a gold rim makes just the right container for a large bunch of sugar-pink roses and paler pink spray carnations. The grey-green foliage of eucalyptus is the perfect foil.*

**1** *Fill a large, round rose bowl with damp foam or crumpled wire if you prefer. Add eucalyptus leaves all over.*

**2** *Next add the spray carnations throughout the foliage, working all round the bowl.*

**3** *Finish by adding all the roses, filling the spaces and making a nice curved outline above the top of the bowl.*

◀ *Roses always make extravagant and beautiful arrangements. During the summer there are plenty of garden varieties to choose from but florist roses are available all the year round. Here pale shell-pink roses combine with lacy umbellifer flowers to make a charming table centrepiece.*

▶ *The miniature roses grown and sold in pots of compost for tubs and containers can easily be transplanted into containers suitable for indoor displays. Here brilliant pink roses look rustic and pretty in a bird's nest basket.*

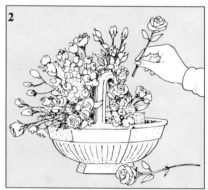

◀ *A flower-decorated pottery basket provides the colour inspiration for this small arrangement of yellow spray rosebuds, cream stock and touches of blue pulmonaria. The buds will slowly open and fill out to completely fill the basket with bloom.*

**1** *Pack the container with damp foam and put the solid heads of stock in place.*

**2** *Add sprays of yellow roses to completely cover the foam and to make a pleasing curving shape a little higher than the handle.*

**3** *Finish off by adding touches of blue flowers in amongst the yellow.*

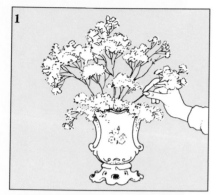

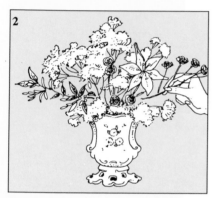

**1** Pack the vase with damp floral foam, bringing it a bit above the top of the container. Place alchemilla throughout.

**2** Add the yellow lily and small sprays of yellow jasmine and purple geraniums, a few sweet peas or something similar.

**3** Finish with the pink and yellow roses, letting one or two bend over. A sprig of convolvulus gives the finishing touch.

◄ *This small arrangement takes its inspiration from the porcelain vase. The painted decoration of pink and yellow garden roses and blue convolvulus are echoed by the real flowers above. Lime green* Alchemilla mollis *makes a superb contrasting background.*

► *A very small and neat arrangement in an unusual colour combination of red, silver and lemon yellow which fits perfectly in the confines of a classic fireplace mantel shelf. It uses mostly garden flowers, with just a few florist's roses in deep, velvety red.*

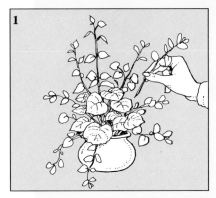

▼ *A small, formal spring arrangement makes use of several different coloured irises available at this time of year. The foliage has been kept to a minimum and consists of long sprays of yew and the ferny leaves of rue. A few golden yellow tulips add highlights of strong colour.*

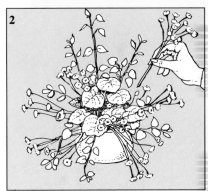

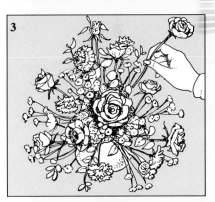

**1** *Pack a small, shallow bowl with damp foam and begin to put the foliage in place.*

**2** *Add the sprays of small yellow santolina button flowers, making a curving outline and facing them all towards the front.*

**3** *Finally put the dahlias in place and then the rose stems, spacing them out well amongst the rest of the material.*

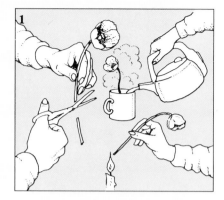

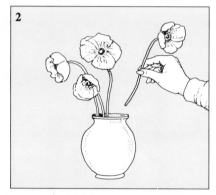

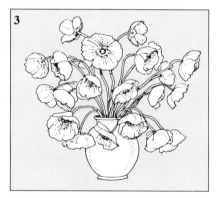

**1** *Poppies need special treatment to last well in water. Cut the stem and either stand in a little boiling water for two minutes or seal over a flame.*

**2** *With their large heads on very delicate stems, poppies can be difficult to arrange. Avoid foam and just stand them in water one at a time.*

**3** *Mix the different colours well and let each flower find its natural position in the container.*

◀ *The simplicity and sparkling colour of Iceland poppies makes them a natural choice to use in a kitchen to add a touch of spice to the surroundings. Here they are simply put in a plain white vase and allowed to glow.*

▶ *Orange and yellow flowers give a wonderful, vibrant effect but are quite hard to arrange successfully. Here the bright orange of lilies and marigolds is tempered by plenty of white feverfew flowers and masses of green filler foliage.*

▼ *A low glass table makes a superb background for a rich mixture of burnt orange gerbera, golden lilies and sprays of euphorbia with bare winter twigs designed to be seen from above and all round.*

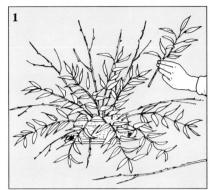

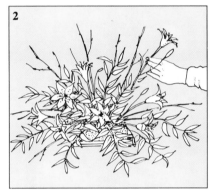

**1** *Put a block of damp foam on a waterproof base and add the foliage, euphorbia and long, bare twigs.*

**2** *Next add the lilies throughout the arrangement, working round in a circle.*

**3** *Finally put in the gerbera daisies, grouping some of them together in a fairly natural way.*

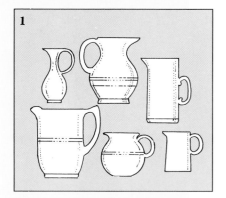

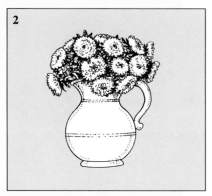

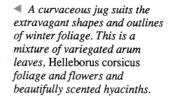

◄ *A curvaceous jug suits the extravagant shapes and outlines of winter foliage. This is a mixture of variegated arum leaves,* Helleborus corsicus *foliage and flowers and beautifully scented hyacinths.*

▶ *Deep coral roses and sprays of garden honeysuckle mix delightfully in a plain and simple green kitchen jug. No mechanics such as foam or wire are needed in a jug as the narrow neck holds flowers in place.*

**1** *Jugs are useful as flower containers. They can be glass, metal or ceramic and can range from the functional to the highly decorative.*

**2** *Informal masses of flowers look best in a jug. They hardly need to be arranged, just put into a bunch and placed in the jug.*

**3** *Take care to get the proportion of flowers to jug right: (left) proportions good, (right) flowers too tall.*

▲ *A slightly more sophisticated arrangement, but the starting point was still a jug, this time an elegant, decorated one. The soft blues, mauves and greens of aquilegia, veronica and chives make a pretty arrangement for a windowsill.*

◄ *Nearly every household has a few different jugs which can be put to use as excellent containers for all kinds of flower arrangements. Jugs always look good and seem to work with many kinds of flowers. Here bold double asters are displayed in a robust blue and cream jug.*

**1** *Fill the jug with water and start by adding stems of honeysuckle of equal length.*

**2** *Next put roses of the same lengths throughout the jug, letting some flop naturally over the edge.*

**3** *Finally finish off by making a small still life with just one stem of honeysuckle and a few pretty objects on the windowsill.*

▼ *A country vaseful of brilliant berries and rosehips waits to be taken indoors. The 30s vase looks superb filled with crab apples, cotoneaster berries, rosehips and bright scarlet pelargonium flowers.*

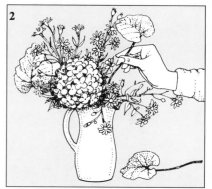

**1** *Fill jug with water and put in the hydrangea flower heads and Michaelmas daisies.*

**2** *Next put in the trailing vine leaves.*

**3** *Finally, add the large sprays of chrysanthemums, balancing them against the weight of the hydrangeas.*

◀ *A very simple jugful of autumn flowers can be turned into something quite special by standing it in amongst a harvest festival of pumpkins and fruit and nuts. The mellow but rich colours of autumn produce are with us only briefly, but should be exploited while they are.*

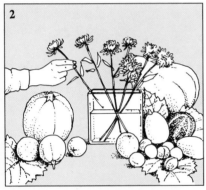

**1** *Stand the tank in position and fill it with water. Put vegetables in place around tank.*

**2** *Put chrysanthemums in the tank, spreading them out quite evenly.*

**3** *Add helichrysums and alstroemeria and spread them throughout the arrangement. Finally re-arrange the vegetables if necessary.*

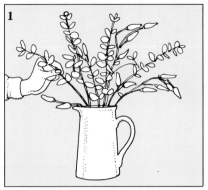

◀ *A golden arrangement to make during the autumn when garden produce is abundant. Chrysanthemums, helichrysums and alstroemeria stand simply in a plain glass tank. The gourds, nuts and pumpkins add colour and interesting shapes to the whole display.*

▶ *The simplest arrangements are often the best. Here a deep green, glossy jug holds a sunshine yellow mixture of ornamental chillies, alstroemeria, helichrysums, chrysanthemums and roses, all set off by a collection of green and yellow gourds.*

**1** *Fill the jug with water and add stems of yellow chillies and eucalyptus leaves.*

**2** *Add stems of alstroemeria, chrysanthemum and helichrysums amongst the foliage.*

**3** *Finally, add the roses, spreading them evenly around the jug.*

# Sweet Simplicity

Many people are nervous about flower arranging, imagining that there are rules to keep and styles to follow. Forget all this and go for something as simple as possible. The ideas in this chapter are perfect for modern interior or period home. What they all have is an elegance that comes from using unfussy containers and simple colour schemes. Bunches of blooms used generously, but with no complicated mechanics, will provide stunning results every time.

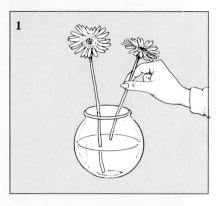

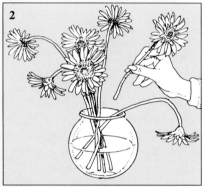

▶ *The strong simplicity of gerbera daisies needs boldly displaying. Try using a simple container such as this round glass gold-fish bowl and be generous in the number of blooms that you use.*

**1** *Make sure that the glass bowl is clean and then fill it with water. Add blooms one at a time.*

**2** *Continue to add single flowers, working round the bowl and filling the gaps. The heads will naturally turn outwards and bend over as they are quite heavy.*

**3** *When you have completely filled the bowl with flowers, finish off by adding several strands of bear grass to curve away from the edge.*

◀ *Highly scented freesias are usually available all the year round and are useful for arranging with other varieties of flower as well as alone, as here, in a simple, rectangular glass vase. Keep the buds opening along the stem by removing faded and dying flowers from the bottom.*

◀ *A pretty wineglass becomes the perfect small-scale container for a simple mixture of garden flowers. The little posy is made up of honeysuckle, lily-of-the-valley, thrift, anemones and hardy geraniums all very casually arranged together.*

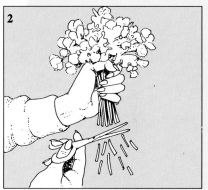

▶ *During the summer months when sweet peas are plentiful they need no other treatment than to be displayed in a plain container such as this clear glass jug. Their scent will fill the whole room and their vibrant mix of strong pastel colours always works well.*

**1** *Make sure the glass jug is very clean and fill it with water. Gather up all the blooms in your hand to make a fat bunch.*

**2** *Cut all the stems to the same length at whatever height is suitable for the container that you have chosen.*

**3** *Still holding the flowers as a bunch, place them in the jug and let them drop. Loosen the flower heads a little if they seem to be too squashed together.*

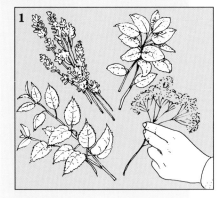

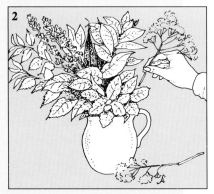

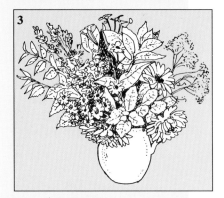

**1** *Begin by picking several different types of herbs. Make each type up into a small bunch of a few stems each.*

**2** *Fill a jug with water and put the bunches of herbs in position.*

**3** *Finish off by putting the marigolds in place round the edge of the jug and amongst the green herbs.*

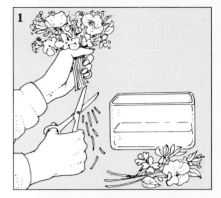

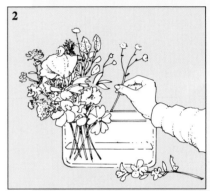

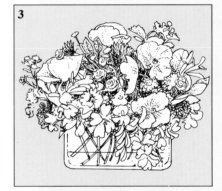

◄ *A bright kitchen windowsill is the home for a rustic pottery jug filled with decorative herbs from the garden. These include variegated mint, feverfew, brilliant orange marigolds, sage leaves, lavender and lemon balm, making a fragrant and colourful arrangement.*

▲ *Brilliant coloured early summer flowers, mainly from the garden, look at their vibrant best generously grouped in a rectangular glass tank. In this case the colour scheme is based on the fact that with flowers anything goes if you are bold enough.*

► *The light, papery texture of Shirley poppy petals is enhanced by the stunning colour range of the flowers. Here long stems are simply arranged in an elegant fluted goblet, silhouetted against a dark background and framed by a small cottage window.*

**1** *Pick and prepare a bunch of mixed garden flowers. Remember that poppies need special treatment . Cut the stems.*

**2** *Beginning at one side of the water-filled tank, put flowers in place, mixing colours and types and facing blooms towards the front.*

**3** *Continue until all the flowers have been used up and you have a solid mass of blooms across the whole tank.*

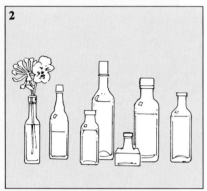

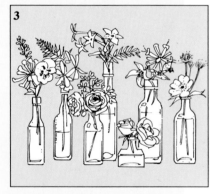

**1** *Collect together a group of small bottles, or you could use glasses, tumblers or small jars.*

**2** *Trim flower stems where necessary and put a single bloom or a bloom and leaf in the first bottle.*

**3** *Continue putting flowers in the bottles until they are all filled and the group looks balanced and complete.*

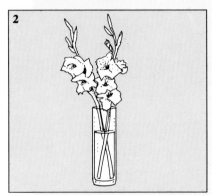

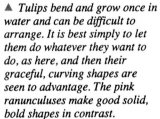

▲ *Tulips bend and grow once in water and can be difficult to arrange. It is best simply to let them do whatever they want to do, as here, and then their graceful, curving shapes are seen to advantage. The pink ranunculuses make good solid, bold shapes in contrast.*

◄ *A good and very easy way to make more of a small amount of material is to isolate each bloom and put them in their own containers. This way you create an important group with maximum effect rather than a single small bunch of mixed flowers.*

► *Tall-stemmed and heavy flowers such as gladioli need special treatment if they are to look good. This tall, clear glass cylinder is solid enough to keep the flowers safe and steady and shows off their handsome stems alongside a few gerberas and anemones.*

**1** *Make sure that the glass container is very clean and three-quarters filled with water. Trim off all the stems, making the two gladioli about the same length.*

**2** *Put the gladioli in first, with the stems leaning towards the front of the vase.*

**3** *Add the gerbera daisies and anemones, filling spaces and making a neat shape.*

67

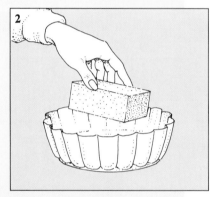

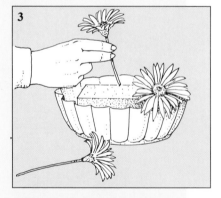

**1** *Search around for all kinds of different containers to inspire your flower arranging. Lots of ordinary everyday objects can easily take on a new lease of life.*

**2** *Put a piece of damp foam into a shallow metal cake mould to hold the flowers in place.*

**3** *Cut the stems of the gerbera quite short and push them into the foam, completely covering the whole surface and mixing the colours evenly.*

▲ *Search kitchen cupboards for unlikely containers for flowers and buy a few things such as this inexpensive shiny tinned cake mould. The sparkle of the silver lifts and brightens the lovely colours of mixed gerberas cut short and arranged thickly.*

◀ *A cheerful and shiny red teapot might not be the obvious choice for a vase, but it works beautifully here with its bright arrangement of orange marigolds, mixed sweet-peas, Shirley poppies and pelargoniums all jumbled together in a riot of summer colour.*

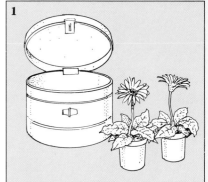

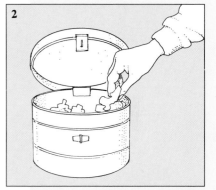

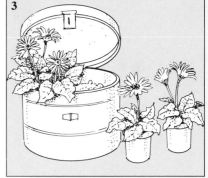

**1** *Empty the box and prop the lid open if necessary.*

**2** *Put crumpled paper or plastic in the base of the box to raise the level of the plants.*

**3** *Simply stand all the pots in the box, mixing the various colours and spacing the blooms out well.*

*A flower arrangement doesn't have to be in water or foam, but instead can consist of a group of growing plants. An old metal hat box with a painted interior to the lid makes a perfect container for pots of growing gerbera.*

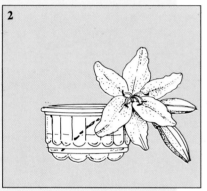

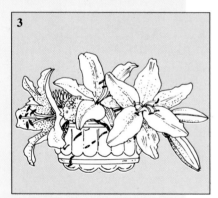

**1** *Prepare three or four lily heads plus any buds they may have. Cut the stems quite short and do the same with the dahlia and chrysanthemum stems.*

**2** *Begin by putting a lily head in place at the side of the container.*

**3** *Add the rest of the lilies one by one, working across the jelly mould. Finally, add the other extra flowers you are using.*

◄ *The fabulous blooms of some scented lilies are cut short and displayed quite plainly with one or two other blooms in an interesting antique glass jelly mould. Nothing else is needed to give this arrangement any more panache.*

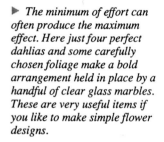

► *The minimum of effort can often produce the maximum effect. Here just four perfect dahlias and some carefully chosen foliage make a bold arrangement held in place by a handful of clear glass marbles. These are very useful items if you like to make simple flower designs.*

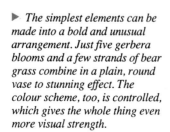

► *The simplest elements can be made into a bold and unusual arrangement. Just five gerbera blooms and a few strands of bear grass combine in a plain, round vase to stunning effect. The colour scheme, too, is controlled, which gives the whole thing even more visual strength.*

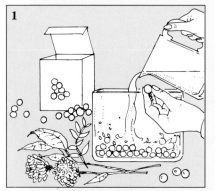

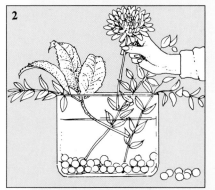

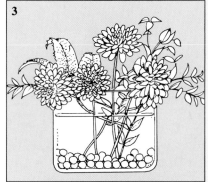

**1** *Begin by gently putting a handful or two of clear glass marbles into a plain glass tank or vase. Add the water.*

**2** *Put about three different bits of foliage in place. Spread them out and leave plenty of space around the leaf shapes. Use the marbles to hold the stems in place. Put in the first bloom.*

**3** *Place three dahlia blooms along the front edge and one a little taller nearer the back of the vase.*

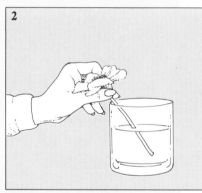

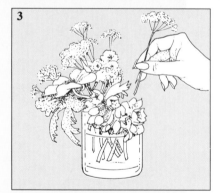

**1** Clean a small tumbler and fill it with water. Collect together several different white flowers and some interesting foliage.

**2** Begin with one leaf and add each piece stem by stem, building up a good mix of leaf and flower.

**3** Keep adding until you have used up all the material or feel that the tumbler looks full enough.

▶ A group of small and simple twigs, flowering shrubs and winter flowers are displayed in a collection of glasses which defines them and makes them more important than if they were massed together in one vase.

◀ In winter months, when flowers are so scarce, even the smallest arrangement can give the greatest pleasure. A few snowdrops picked from the garden look best displayed in a tiny container which does not detract from their fresh white and green.

▼ An octagonal drinking tumbler is used to hold a collection of white and green flowers and foliage including lace flower, chincherinchees, poppy seed heads and anemones. It would make a perfect decoration at a bedside or for a dining table.

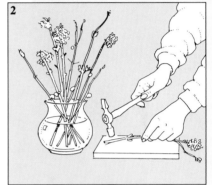

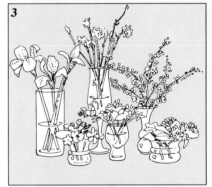

**1** *Collect together a group of small glasses both stemmed and plain. Fill them with water and stand them in a group.*

**2** *Prepare any woody twigs by hammering or splitting the ends of the stems. Make small bunches of all the different garden material collected.*

**3** *Put the small bunches of each variety into separate glasses, balancing heights and colours to make a harmonious group.*

# Clever Centrepieces

Good food deserves beautiful flowers to set the scene. A dining table, whether set for a quick breakfast or a leisurely dinner, looks finished and inviting with some kind of flower centrepiece. Flowers can be chosen to complement or contrast with the food, to echo a colour in plates or table linen, or simply to work within the whole room. Bear in mind that people need room to eat and to see and talk easily to other guests. Keep centrepieces fairly low and though fragrant flowers are pleasing, choose nothing too scented which might clash with the food.

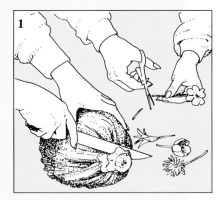

**1** *Prepare the ornamental cabbage by removing any damaged or dirty outside leaves and cutting the base off the stem so that the cabbage will stand safely.*

**2** *Cut the stems of the flowers quite short and tuck them in amongst the layers of leaves.*

**3** *Continue adding flower heads until the cabbage looks pretty. Stand the cabbage on a plate or mat to protect the surface under it.*

◀ A decorative pink and green ornamental cabbage becomes the focus of a pretty table arrangement. As it has to last only a short time, the flowers are simply put in amongst the leaves and will look good for a few hours while the meal takes place.

▶ A prettily speckled summer squash has been hollowed out to hold a bunch of summer annuals. As long as a certain thickness of fruit is left inside the skin, a squash is quite waterproof and makes an excellent container for flowers. Stand it on a mat or plate to avoid staining precious furniture.

▼ A small golden pumpkin makes a rustic container for bright, glowing orange and yellow marigolds from the garden. Fruit and vegetables make ideal material for arrangements destined for a dining table.

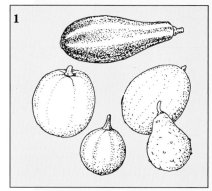

**1** All kinds of small squashes, melons and pumpkins can be used as flower containers as long as they are firm and sound.

**2** Take a thin slice off the bottom of the fruit so that it will stand up. Slice off the top and discard.

**3** With a sharp-edged spoon, scoop out plenty of flesh, leaving enough to make a waterproof shell.

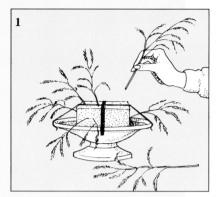

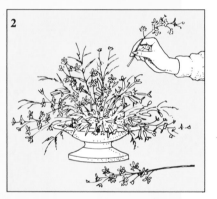

**1** Tape a block of damp foam onto a shallow dish or container. Add branches of foliage all over the foam.

**2** Add sprays of Michaelmas daisies and euphorbia throughout the foliage, aiming for an all round effect and regular shape.

**3** Finish by putting stems of spray carnations throughout the arrangement, making sure that they are evenly distributed.

▲ A formal dinner setting demands flowers to match. On a richly polished dining table the spray carnations and starry Michaelmas daisies are light and elegant without taking any emphasis away from gleaming glasses and sparkling cutlery.

▶ A sophisticated colour theme for a simple buffet meal. The madras check cloth inspires a mix of peach-coloured flowers including exotic protea, lilies, roses and chrysanthemums. The effect is casual and fun, to suit the mood of the party.

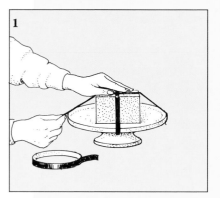

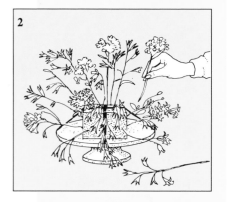

▲ *An arrangement for late summer is made using a mass of orange lilies, alstroemeria, roses, spray carnations and chrysanthemums, with branches of tiny, bright rosehips to add extra spice to the colour scheme. A perfect design for a side table or dining table.*

▶ *A classic and elegant arrangement made on a low, stemmed fruit dish. The sweetness of so much pink is counteracted by the deeper tones of the Stargazer lilies and the touches of pale blue from the drooping bells of brodiaea.*

**1** *Tape a block of damp foam to a low compotier or similar dish.*

**2** *Put stems of brodiaea and euphorbia in place first all over the foam.*

**3** *Next put the large lily blooms in place and then finish off with the spray carnations.*

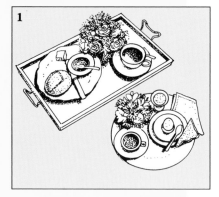

◄ *Bright and cheerful mixed flowers echo the floral tray that they stand on. A few stems cut short can simply be put in an egg cup or some other small-scale container beside the breakfast egg and toast.*

**1** *Any tray, whether it is for supper by the fire or a special meal for an invalid, looks extra special with flowers added.*

**2** *The simplest arrangement for a tray is a small bunch made in the hand and put into a container which will not take up too much room.*

**3** *Alternatively, a small arrangement of dried flowers can be put into a foam base to decorate a tray.*

▶ *Supper by the fire and a tiny arrangement of poppy seed heads, euonymous berries, polygonum spikes and alstroemeria make a carefully chosen decoration for the tray.*

▶ *A healthy breakfast on a tray looks even more appetising with a pretty winter posy of dried flowers alongside it. Here small florets of greenish hydrangea are mixed with helichrysums and dried* Alchemilla mollis *on a colour co-ordinated tray.*

▼ *Breakfast in bed is a great way to start the day, especially when it is accompanied by a posy of flowers fresh from the garden. Love-in-a-mist and pinks mixed with scented honeysuckle shows that someone really cares.*

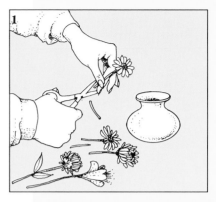

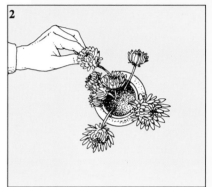

▶ *An individual arrangement beside a table setting is charming and shows thought for a guest. It can be as simple and quick as a few stems of fragrant freesias casually arranged in a glass tumbler.*

**1** *Find a small container to fit the tray and fill it with water. Cut stems of flowers short enough to fit.*

**2** *Put chrysanthemum heads in place first all round the container.*

**3** *Next add alstroemeria and Michaelmas daisies throughout the arrangement.*

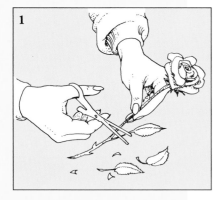

**1** Clean and polish the goblet and fill with water. Collect several different types of roses.

**2** Trim off the rose thorns and leaves and cut the stems at a slant.

**3** Fill the goblet with roses one by one.

▲ *A romantic dinner outdoors needs special flowers to complete the high summer theme. A tall glass goblet is simply filled with several different varieties of old-fashioned garden roses, richly coloured and strongly perfumed.*

◄ *A warm summer afternoon and a very English tea of bread and strawberry jam and strawberry tartlets is set off by a brimming basketful of garden flowers such as jasmine, roses, pelargoniums, geums and alpine strawberries.*

► *A simple iced sponge cake has its own flower arrangement which is designed in this case to look pretty but not to be eaten. The jugful of garden flowers combines the rich summer colour of cornflowers, sweet peas and roses.*

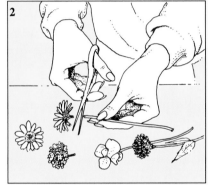

**1** *Assemble a mixture of different flowers. Make sure the cake icing has set and is hard enough to put flowers on. Stand the cake on a plate with space for the flowers.*

**2** *Cut the stems off the flowers leaving just the heads for the decoration of the plate.*

**3** *Lay the flowers in a circle round the edge of the plate. Make a small group of flowers in the centre of the cake.*

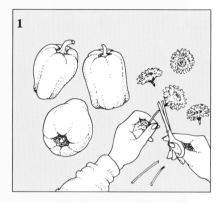

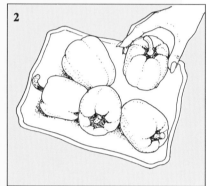

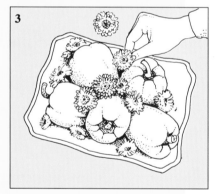

**1** Choose a group of sound and fresh sweet peppers. Snip the stems off the flower heads.

**2** Lay the peppers out on a shallow rectangular plate.

**3** Scatter the fresh flower heads in amongst the peppers.

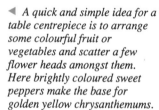

▶ An alfresco breakfast complete with brioche, croissants and a jug of orange juice is made even more enjoyable by a basket of brilliant, sunny coloured flowers on the green metal garden table under the vine. It hardly matters whether the sun shines or not.

◀ A tablecloth can often be the starting point or inspiration for a table arrangement. This fresh, sunny combination of acid green and yellow is highlighted by a posy of lilies, alstroemeria and chrysanthemums.

◀ A quick and simple idea for a table centrepiece is to arrange some colourful fruit or vegetables and scatter a few flower heads amongst them. Here brightly coloured sweet peppers make the base for golden yellow chrysanthemums.

◀ A simple, crisp and fresh basket of wildflowers complements an outdoor lunch. The natural colour scheme of white, yellow and green comes from a casual arrangement of buttercups and daisies.

**1** *Find a waterproof container which will stand hidden in the basket. Fill the inner pot with water.*

**2** *Begin to put stems of small-flowered daisies into the container and then add buttercups.*

**3** *Finally add the larger white daisies evenly throughout the arrangement.*

# Perfect Posies

A tiny handful of simple wild flowers or a large bunch of glamorous blooms – however you make a posy, the results are bound to please. Posies are one of the simplest ways to arrange flowers and they make an ideal gift for all kinds of occasions. Traditionally, posies are carried by a bride and her attendants and in Victorian times were given as love tokens and taken to grand balls and parties as decoration for beautiful gowns. A well-made posy can be stood in water as a ready-made flower arrangement.

**1** *Collect several different varieties of herb from the garden, including some that are in flower.*

**2** *Make a posy and trim the stems to the same length. Put a rubber band round the stems to hold them in place.*

**3** *Tie a ribbon or decorative tape around the rubber band, and if it is a gift attach a label too. Several such bunches would look good in a small basket.*

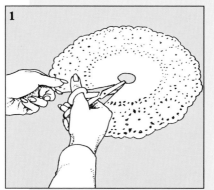

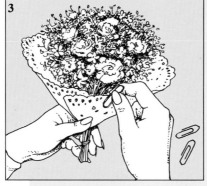

◀ *Little posies of fresh garden herbs make the most delightful gift or instant bouquet. Several bunches in a bowl in the kitchen look pretty and might provide inspiration and delicious ingredients for a keen cook. Many herbs have the bonus of pretty flowers too.*

▲ *A delightful small posy which would make a perfect arrangement for a small bridesmaid to carry. Framed by a paper lace collar, the bunch contains annual gypsophila, lime green Alchemilla mollis and Doris pinks.*

**1** *Cut into the centre of a paper doiley and cut a small circle of paper out from the middle.*

**2** *Make a hand-held posy of mixed flowers and tie the stems tightly in place with wire, thread or a rubber band.*

**3** *Wrap the doiley around the flowers making a cone shape. Overlap the cut edges slightly and secure in place with a paperclip.*

**1**

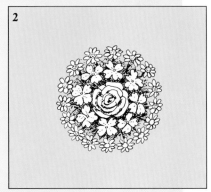

**2**

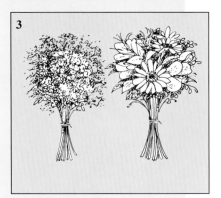

**3**

**1** *To make a formal Victorian-style posy of concentric rings of different colours and flowers, begin with a single central flower then add the first ring of flowers round it.*

**2** *Make more rings round this using different types of flowers and/or colours. Build up circles until the posy is the right size.*

**3** *Finish off the posy with a neat collar of matching leaves in a contrasting colour.*

90

◀ *It takes very little time and is great fun to create several very different posies from garden flowers. Years ago these little bunches were known as tussie-mussies and were carried as a protection against disease and to mask unpleasant smells.*

▼ *A bold colour scheme of yellow, white and blue which includes yellow jasmine revolutum, deep blue annual cornflowers, yellow marigolds, lavender, pale lemon achillea and the soft green seed heads of Shirley poppies. A few variegated leaves add substance.*

◀ *Deep pinks and reds combine to make a beautiful, richly coloured posy. The dusky reddish leaves of purple sage set off brilliant pelargonium flowers and spikes of polygonum. There are small fuchsia flowers too and delicate astrantia blooms like tiny pin cushions.*

▼ *Sprigs of bright green curled parsley complement the gleaming colours of kitchen garden marigolds and nasturtiums. This little posy would last surprisingly well in water and cheer up any room which needed it.*

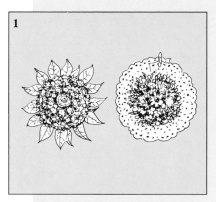

**1**

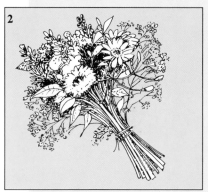

**2**

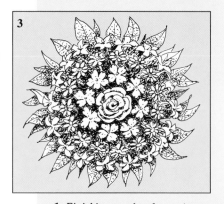

**3**

**1** *Finishing touches for posies can include a paper doiley frill or collar round the edge, or any kind of decorative leaf.*

**2** *Mixed posies can be simple creations with the flowers arranged at random.*

**3** *You can use the basic method of making a posy to create quite large bunches. In this case use larger flowers, which show up well. Small posies demand small and dainty ingredients.*

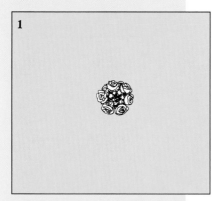

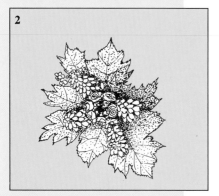

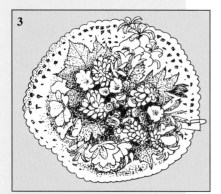

**1** *Begin with the central flower, in this case a sprig of double perennial wallflowers.*

**2** *Add a few grape hyacinths and some foliage, holding the posy in your hand and working round it.*

**3** *Add primroses and other small flowers, mixing in more leaves as you go. Finally, make a paper collar and wrap it round the posy. Secure the stems tightly.*

▲ *Another posy made from spring flowers exploits the fresh colours of this season. Little clusters of blue grape hyacinths are mixed with pale yellow primroses, wallflowers, sweet violets and white pulmonaria flowers. Fresh green foliage is important to separate the different colours from each other.*

▶ *A carefully chosen mixture of flowers makes a delightful posy to give as a present. One beautiful coral rose provides the centrepiece, surrounded by deep purple sage leaves, starry London Pride, polygonum spikes, pink spray carnations and pelargonium flowers. A rich gold doiley looks splendid surrounding the posy.*

◀ *A brilliant mixture of colours combine in this posy made from spring flowers. There are purple aquilegia, yellow buttercups, pink wallflowers and variegated foliage all set off by a crisp white paper doiley collar.*

# Beautiful Baskets

*Baskets have always seemed a natural and highly suitable container to present flowers in. The subtle browns and beiges and interesting textures of the vast range now available, from rough and twisted to smooth and glossy, make a perfect background to the delicate petals and glowing colours of flowers and foliage. If you intend to use a basket for fresh flowers which need water then you will have to use an inner container, or take advantage of the easy-to-use floral foams, which are ideal for this particular method of display.*

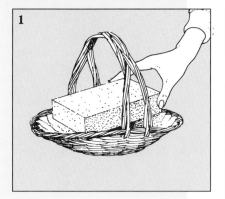

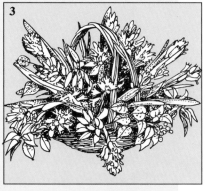
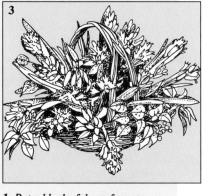

**1** Put a block of damp foam to fit tightly in the lined basket.

**2** Cover the foam all over with sprays of ivy, letting some hang over the edge of the basket.

**3** Put a mixture of pink and white hyacinth stems throughout the ivy, aiming for an all round effect.

◀ *A pretty, handled basket needs the simplest treatment to show it off best. Here pink and white hyacinths are combined generously and arranged in a mass of glossy dark green evergreen ivy leaves. The scent is soft and gentle and very evocative of spring.*

▶ *A fresh and simple spring arrangement full of colour and scent. The bold, dark green foliage offsets pale lemon freesias and narcissi and contrasting pink is provided by stems of hyacinths and many petalled ranunculuses, all arranged in a very casual way in a pale cane basket.*

▶ *An arrangement for late winter, when the first hyacinths and ranunculuses are in the flower shops and there is the start of a supply of foliage from the garden to put with them. Stems of scented viburnum and the subtle, speckled heads of hellebores add interest.*

**1** *Put a block of damp foam in a deep, lined basket. Cover the foam with foliage.*

**2** *Next add the stems of hyacinth evenly throughout the foliage.*

**3** *Finally, add the stems of freesia and ranunculus, letting a few curve downwards over the edge of the basket.*

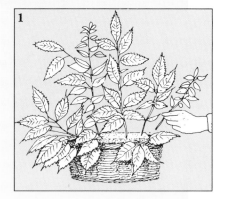

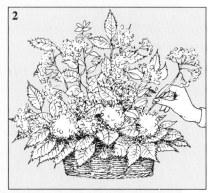

**1** *Pack blocks of damp foam into the lined baskets. Working on both baskets, begin by putting stems of foliage in place, tall stems at the back, short ones along the front edge.*

**2** *Put the large blooms, such as hydrangeas, in place and then sprays of lace flower.*

**3** *Finish by putting in stems of anemones, alstroemeria and roses.*

◀ *A pair of magnificent baskets spilling over with beautiful flowers. Using two arrangements gives an air of formality, but the flowers themselves are almost rustic. The strong shapes of sweet chestnut leaves give form and texture to the whole design.*

▼ *Using a heart-shaped basket (see overleaf) makes putting together a special Valentine's Day gift very easy. Here scented white lilac, single white daisies and apricot carnations have been arranged around golden yellow rosebuds.*

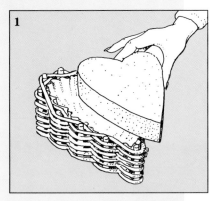

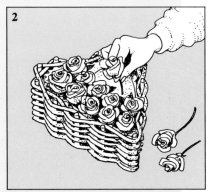

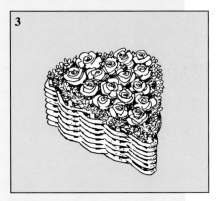

**1** *Cut the foam to fit neatly into a lined basket. Soak the foam and pack it into the basket.*

**2** *Put central flowers such as roses in place first, arranging them in a heart shape.*

**3** *Put lilac, or whatever you are using, round the roses, completely filling the basket. No foam should show at all.*

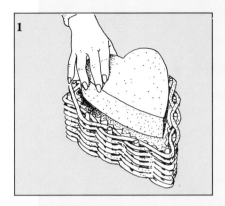

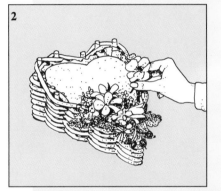

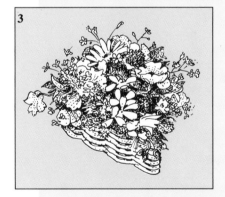

◄ *This arrangement has the feel of an old Victorian Valentine to it, and even if modern florist's roses are not scented the lilac should make up for this.*

▲ *A lot of thought has gone into the choice of flowers and colours used in this heart-shaped basket filled from the garden. Aquilegias have been combined with fluffy saxifrage, and bright pelargonium flowers sit beside soft mauve chive blooms and pale anemones.*

**1** *Cut the foam to fit a lined basket. Soak the foam and pack it into place.*

**2** *Using a variety of mixed flowers, push the stems into the foam, packing the flowers together closely and working across the whole area of foam.*

**3** *Complete the arrangement by adding flowers all over the foam and allowing some flowers to hang slightly over the edges of the basket.*

**1** Either buy a basket that is already lined, or line one of your own with strong plastic sheet.

**2** Take plants from pots and put several into the basket, packing them quite close together.

**3** When the basket is full of iris, push moss around their stems to completely cover the potting compost.

◄ *A finely woven, glossy basket in a rich toffee brown is the perfect foil for spikes of deep purple* Iris reticulata. *Bought as small pot plants, they have been replanted into the lined basket and will be planted indoors when flowering has finished.*

► *This basket arrangement of brilliant colours makes clever use of small pots of growing primroses, which can be bought readily and cheaply in late winter and early spring. They are packed quite tightly into a low, oval basket and any gaps are concealed with moss.*

**1** Either buy a ready-lined basket or carefully line one of your own with plastic sheet. Fill the basket up to the top with damp foam.

**2** Cover the top of the foam with fresh green moss and begin to put the first few twigs in place. Vary the height of the twigs for a natural look.

**3** Follow up by adding stems of daffodils. Use buds and flowers, again at different heights and facing in different directions.

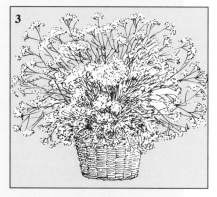

**1** Find a large, stable, waterproof container such as a glass jar which will stand hidden inside the basket. Fill it with water.

**2** Begin to fill the jar randomly with the sprays of flowers, working all round to fill the jar and spacing the blooms out either side of the handle.

**3** Continue filling the jar with stems until the basket looks full and generous.

▲ *A cool white and green early-summer arrangement in a low willow basket which includes long spikes of rich green fern, soft white foxgloves, meadow grasses, white long-stemmed roses and Alchemilla mollis foliage and flowers.*

◀ *Spectacular simplicity is achieved by filling a large, pale willow shopping basket with armfuls of snowy white Queen Anne's lace (cow parsley) – a perfect solution to camouflaging an empty fireplace, or for any dark corner that needs a lift.*

▶ *A small-scale arrangement of different culinary herbs shows what a range and variety there is in their leaf colours, textures and markings. The subtle mixture includes mint, golden marjoram, fennel, rue, rosemary, feverfew, sweet woodruff, alpine strawberry and chive flowers.*

**1** *For a shallow basket arrangement use damp foam to hold the flowers in place. Buy a ready-lined basket, or line it yourself with plastic or metal foil.*

**2** *Work across the foam, putting stems in place starting in the middle and moving out either side. Aim for a smooth, neat, hummock-shaped outline to the flowers and foliage.*

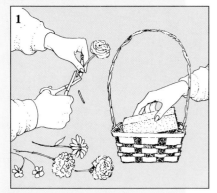

**1** *Have ready a collection of dried flowers and leaves. Cut them short, leaving only a short piece of stem.*

**2** *Begin by gluing leaves across the front edge and a few over the handle.*

**3** *Build up the rest of the design using a mixture of other dried flowers, balancing shapes and colours amongst the whole arrangement.*

▼ *A specially designed flat basket to hold a dried flower arrangement. The flowers should be glued into place, preferably with a glue gun. Included in this mixture are roses, helichrysums, love-in-a-mist, carthamnus and glycerined leaves, in a strong colour scheme of orange and yellow.*

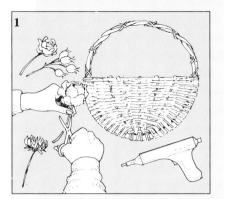

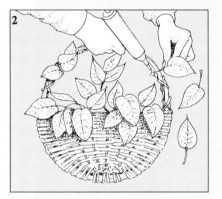

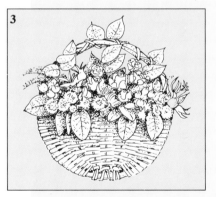

**1** *Have ready a collection of dried flowers and leaves. Cut them short, leaving only a short piece of stem.*

**2** *Begin by gluing leaves across the front edge and a few over the handle.*

**3** *Build up the rest of the design using a mixture of other dried flowers, balancing shapes and colours amongst the whole arrangement.*

◀ *Woven stained natural wood and bright plastic combine to make a pretty basket which, filled with flowers, makes an ideal gift. The tall handle makes it easy to carry. Choose simple flowers, such as single daisies and spray carnations, to fit with the style of the basket.*

# Garlands & Wreaths

In recent years we have become used to seeing garlands and wreaths at all times of the year. At one time circlets of evergreens were commonly used to decorate houses at Christmas, but now there are few occasions when wreaths and garlands would not fit in. A wreath can be made on a damp foam or moss base, or dried flowers can be attached to straw, foam or twig rings. Quick and easy wreaths can be put together on a ring of woven vine branches or just on wire alone. Imagination is the only limitation.

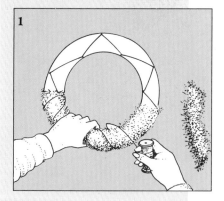

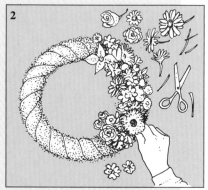

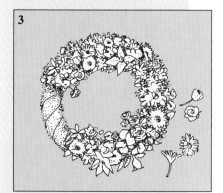

▶ *This garland was made by putting short-stemmed flowers into a damp foam wreath base. It is ideal for fresh flowers, which will last like this for several days. Lots of different species of flower have been combined to colourful effect here, including clematis, marigolds, roses, geraniums, sweet peas, geums and nasturtiums.*

**1** *Begin with a wire frame. Wrap moss round the frame and wire it into place with thin rose wire.*

**2** *Completely cover the frame with moss, then begin to add flowers and leaves, pushing the stems into the moss. Wire some secure if necessary.*

**3** *Continue working right round the frame until it is completely covered with flowers. Spray with a mist of water to keep it fresh.*

◀ *A light and bright summer garland made from daisies, jasmine, feverfew, cornflowers, variegated mint leaves, love-in-a-mist and golden yellow achillea. Strong colours always look fresh if they are mixed with plenty of white for contrast.*

▶ *Full-flowered summer roses are the focus for this beautiful garland. To add to the fragrance, sweet peas are included too, and old-fashioned veronica and astrantia are twinned throughout the circle. It looks lovely on a mellow stone wall, but would look equally good on a door or wall indoors.*

**1** *A slightly different approach to making a wreath is first to cover the frame completely with leaves or filler material.*

**2** *Add single flowers of the same type at regular intervals right round the frame.*

**3** *Finish by filling between main flowers with other small flowers or little bunches of blooms.*

# Garlands & Wreaths

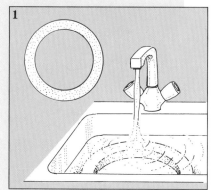

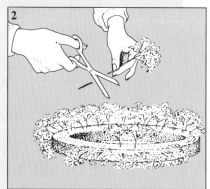

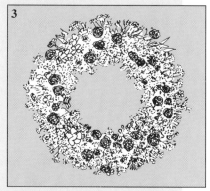

**1** Soak the foam base in a large bowl or sink. Refer to manufacturers' instructions as to how long this should be for.

**2** Cut stems short on the filler material so that you have plenty. Begin to cover the foam with the flowers.

**3** Add the small flower heads and other materials, scattering them evenly throughout. Make sure the inner edges of the ring are well hidden.

◄ This frothy wreath is made with a base of delicate Alchemilla mollis *flowers. Tucked in amongst this are small, purple hardy geranium flowers and sweet peas. Tiny pieces of green sedum and stokesia flower heads complete the picture.*

▶ *Marigolds and nasturtiums are both culinary flowers, being used to add colour and flavour to food, particularly salads. Combined here along with* Alchemilla mollis *they make a delightful countrified garland. Golden marjoram leaves add a note of bright green and a sweet herbal scent.*

▼ *A cool and sparkling green and white garland made from late summer garden flowers. The background is steely blue rue foliage and added to this are white hydrangeas, scented jasmine, sweet peas, and veronica. Always take care when handling rue, as the juice from the stems can irritate skin that is later exposed to sunlight.*

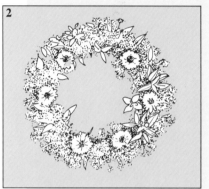

**1** Soak a foam ring base and attach a wire or some other means of hanging it later. Cover the whole ring with foliage and filler until the foam is hidden.

**2** Add the marigold flowers throughout, spacing them evenly round the circle.

**3** Add the nasturtiums and other smaller flowers in a more random pattern until the whole appears well balanced.

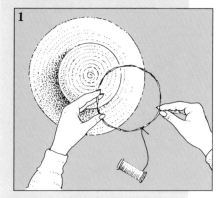

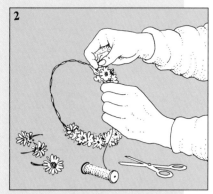

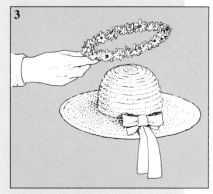

◄ A child's straw hat makes a perfect base for a pretty dried flower decoration. The flowers can be wired onto a circlet around the crown, or more permanently glued into place. Here the big red bow sets off the bright helichrysums and helipterums, and adds definition and a sense of fun.

► A small-scale wreath made from dried flowers. An arrangement like this one can be created using a home-made straw base or a ready-made foam ring. Included in this version are golden yellow helichrysums, achillea flower heads and silvery sea lavender. A little deep brown foliage sets off the light colours well and the silky ribbon adds a lovely finishing touch.

**1** Make a wire circle to fit loosely over the crown of the hat. Twist the ends together and remove from hat.

**2** Wire short-stemmed flower heads to the circlet, working in one direction right round the circle until you have a wreath of flowers.

**3** Slide the finished ring over the hat crown and pin or wire it into place. Wire a bow in position to finish off.

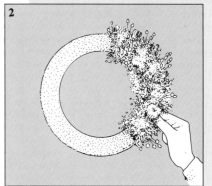

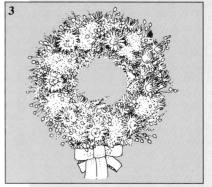

**1** You will need a dry foam ring and flower material with stems cut short. Some flowers with soft stems may need to be wired.

**2** Begin to cover the foam ring with a base of filler material. Work all around until the ring is covered.

**3** Add single flower heads throughout the base covering, keeping the spacing between flowers fairly even and the colours well balanced.

115

# Flowers to Last

Dried flowers are a wonderful way of bringing colour to a house in winter, when fresh flowers are scarce and expensive, or for rooms that are just not suitable for any other kind of decoration. Warm, centrally heated houses mean that fresh flowers last only a short time, so dried flowers have really come into their own. The choice is huge and the colour range exciting and there are dried decoration ideas to suit every taste and type of interior.

**1** Wedge blocks of dry floral foam into base of the basket, making them level with the top edge.

**2** Cover foam completely with a filler such as sea lavender.

**3** Continue filling the basket, now using a mixture of other flowers and leaves. Aim to make a slightly domed outline.

▲ A large, rectangular basket made from sturdy twigs and with a stout handle makes a good container for a subtle mix of different dried flowers and leaves, including poppy seed heads, helichrysums, roses, sorrel, marigolds and amaranthus.

◀ This two-colour basket, with its elegant, twisted handle and lavender edging, contains another rich mixture of many different dried flowers. Helichrysums and deep red dahlias mix with love-in-a-mist and grey sea lavender. The effect relies on texture and colour, like the rug it sits on.

▶ Sparkling helichrysums fresh from harvesting are bright and shiny. The colours fade only very slowly if they are kept from strong sunlight. Used alone in a colourful mass, helichrysums are very effective.

**1** *Put dry foam in the base of the basket.*

**2** *Prepare flowers. Helichrysums will need to be wired. This is best done when they are fresh, but can be done once dry. Push a stub wire down through the centre of the bloom. Make a hook in the top end, which lodges into the flower head.*

**3** *Fill whole basket with flowers, working across and making a neat, dense arrangement.*

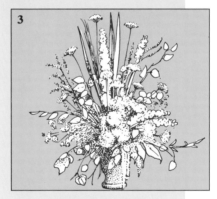

**1** *Begin by putting the bold-shaped foliage in place first.*

**2** *Continue with the other foliage and material, filling in spaces and keeping an overall triangular outline in mind*

**3** *Finish off with the achillea and orange lanterns as the focal points.*

*A collection of dried and preserved autumn flowers and foliage with a simple country feel. The beech leaves, molucella and fatsia leaves have been preserved in glycerine, which gives them a soft sheen. In contrast, the brilliant orange physalis lanterns and golden achillea glow warmly in a plain and simple setting.*

The strong shapes of ornamental chillies are highlighted against a
cottage window. The silvery seed covers of honesty come alive with
the light shining through them and contrast with the heavy
ears of wheat.

**1** Put the fresh evergreen foliage
in first, then add the honesty seed
heads. You may need dry foam
depending on your container.

**2** Add the sprays of chilli
peppers next, making the outline
they create the furthest extent of
the space they take up.

**3** Finally add the stems of wheat
and let them droop and curve
downwards.

▲ *An unusual mixture of colours for a dried arrangemment works very well here against the complementary backdrop of a deep blue and yellow rug. Dark blue larkspur and lavender are used with achillea, marigolds, poppy heads and soft green grasses.*

**1** *Pack dry foam into basket of your choice, keeping top of foam level with top of basket.*

**2** *Make small bunches, if neccessary, of any small-scale flowers and tie with wire. Push into foam along with filler material. Work across basket.*

**3** *Fill whole basket with bunches and single flowers until you have a dense, neat mass of flowers.*

▶ *A gentle arrangement in peach and terracotta colours spills out from a shallow basket. Statice in several similar shades is put together with dried roses, santolina flowers and sprays of sea lavender.*

**1** *Tape foam into shallow basket, slicing it lower if required.*

**2** *Fill in outline with statice and leaves, making a spreading triangular shape.*

**3** *Finish off with helichrysums and dried roses spread throughout the statice.*

123